Totline "Take-Home" Books
Object Rhymes

Reproducible Pre-Reading Books
For Young Children

Written by Jean Warren • Illustrated by Barb Tourtillotte

Editorial Staff: Gayle Bittinger, Elizabeth McKinnon, Susan M. Sexton, Jean Warren
Production Director: Eileen Carbary
Design: Kathy Jones
Cover-Computer Graphics: Kathy Jones & Eric Stovall
Inside Pages-Text and Computer Graphics: André Gene Samson

ISBN 0-911019-33-2

Printed in the United States of America
Published by: Warren Publishing House, Inc.
             P.O. Box 2250
             Everett, WA 98203

20 19 18 17 16 15 14 13 12 11 10 9 8 7 6 5 4

CONTENTS

Fall Object Books
Leaves Everywhere
Pumpkins Everywhere
Turkeys Everywhere

Winter Object Books
Bows Everywhere
Snow Everywhere
Hearts Everywhere

Spring Object Books
Shamrocks Everywhere
Rain Everywhere
Flowers Everywhere

Summer Object Books
Butterflies Everywhere
Flags Everywhere
Sand Everywhere

Introduction

Young children who are just becoming interested in books and reading are usually long on enthusiasm and short on ability. Totline "Take-Home" Books are designed to capture that enthusiasm.

Each of the pre-reading books in Object Rhymes centers around a seasonal theme and is written in rhyme. The unique feature of these rhymes is that young children are able to "read" them, using pictures as their guides. This happens because each rhyme is simply written and illustrated with pre-readers in mind. After reading a book with an adult a few times, your children will be able to "read" it by themselves.

Because all of the pre-reading books in this series are reproducible, your children can each have his or her own. And they will glow with pride and feelings of accomplishment as they take home their own books to "read" to their families.

General Directions

- Tear out the pages for the take-home book of your choice.

- Make one photocopy of the book for each child. Cut the pages in half.

- Place the pages on a table and let the children help collate them into books.

- Give each child two 5 1/2- by 8-inch pieces of construction paper to use for book covers.

- Let the children decorate their book covers as desired or use one of the suggestions on the following pages.

- Help the children bind their books using a stapler or a hole punch and brass paper fasteners.

Suggestions for Using the
Objects Rhymes
Take-Home Books

• The take-home books in *Object Rhymes* are fun and easy to use. You can enlarge the pages to make big books for your room, introduce the rhymes with flannelboard cutouts or give out books at the end of a unit. Following are some ideas for using the take-home books with preschoolers, kindergartners and first and second graders. Mix and match the ideas to meet the needs and interests of your children.

Preschool

• Let the children use rubber stamps that correspond with the rhyme's subject to stamp the covers of their books.

• Give the children appropriate stickers to attach to the covers of their books.

• Cut sponges into appropriate seasonal shapes. Let the children use the sponges like stamps to print designs on their book covers.

• Make paint pads by folding paper towels, placing them in shallow containers and pouring small amounts of tempera paint on them. Give the children cookie cutters in the appropriate shapes. Have them dip their cookie cutters into the paint and then press them on the covers of their books.

• Add extra pages to the end of each book. Cut out seasonal magazine pictures that relate to the rhyme. Have the children glue them to their extra pages. Ask them to name or describe the objects when they read their books.

• Photocopy each half page on a separate page. Cut the pages into an appropriate shape.

Kindergarten

• Let the children cut out and glue magazine pictures of the appropriate season on their book covers.

• Have the children write their names on the backs of their books.

• Have the children color just the seasonal objects on the pages in the book.

First and Second Grades

• Let the children take their books home to color.

• Have the children write "This book belongs to (child's name)" on their back covers.

• Have the children copy each sentence of a particular rhyme onto a separate page. Let them illustrate each of their pages.

• Photocopy each half page on a full sheet of paper with lines for writing below the picture. Have the children copy the words on the pages.

• Add extra pages to the back of each child's book. Let the children cut out appropriate magazine pictures and glue them to the pages. Have the children write the names of the objects below them.

• Have the children draw the picture of things that correspond to the rhyme on the covers of their books.

• Let the children create book covers by drawing pictures of things they like to do in the appropriate season.

Fall
Books

Leaves on the pumpkin.

Leaves on the tree.

Leaves on the house.

Leaves on me.

Leaves on the ground.

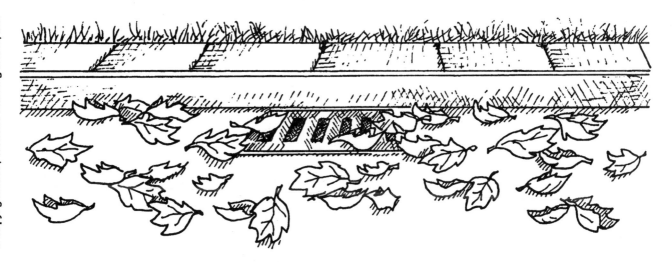

Leaves on the street.

Leaves on the car.

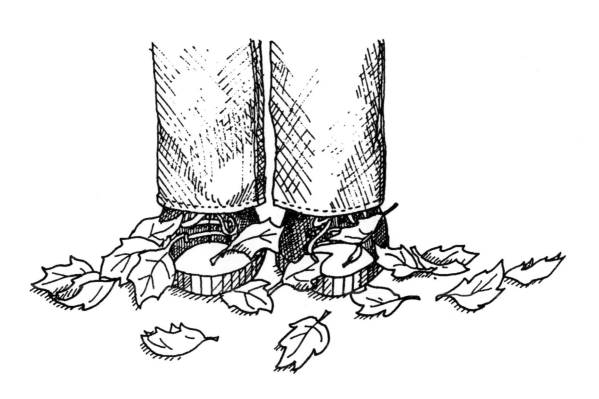

Leaves on the feet.

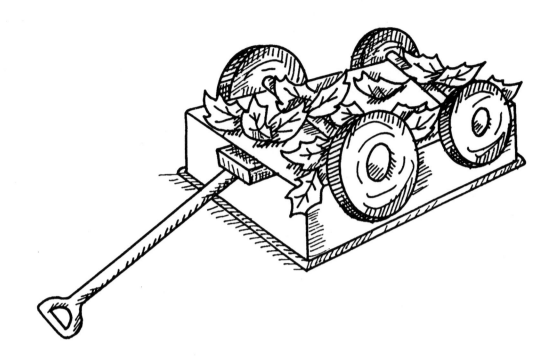

Leaves on the wagon.

Leaves on the bear.

Leaves on the dog.

Leaves everywhere!

Pumpkins by the barn.

Pumpkins by the house.

Pumpkins by the wagon.

Pumpkins by the mouse.

Pumpkins by the fence.

Pumpkins by the cat.

Pumpkins by the scarecrow.

Pumpkins by the hat.

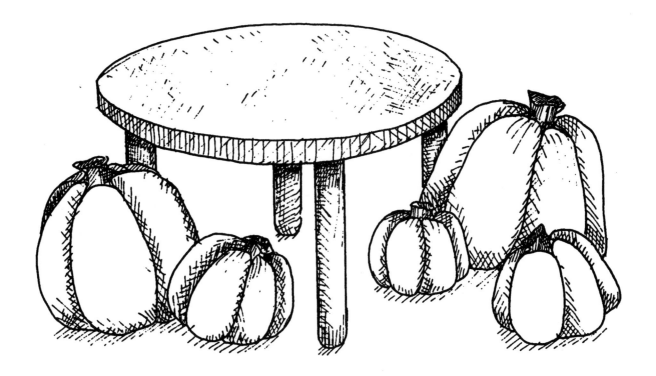

Pumpkins by the table.

Pumpkins by the chair.

Pumpkins by the door.

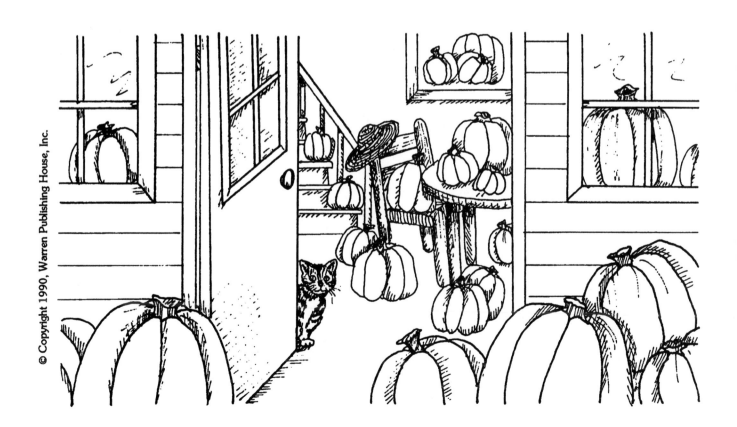

Pumpkins everywhere!

Turkeys by the pumpkins.

Turkeys by the well.

Turkeys by the haystack.

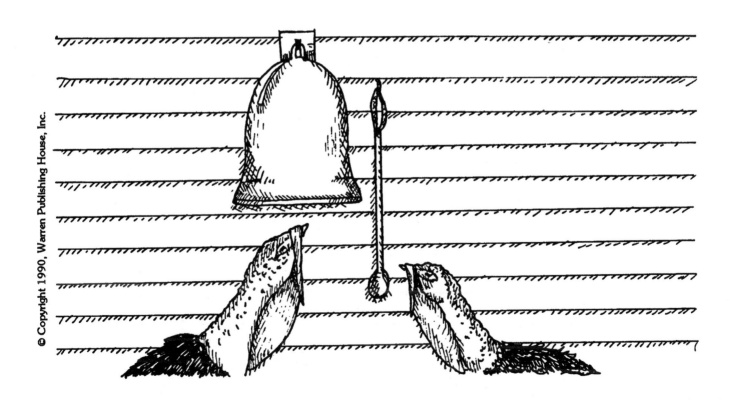

Turkeys by the bell.

Turkeys by the barn.

Turkeys by the corn.

Turkeys by the wagon.

Turkeys by the horn.

Turkeys by the wheel.

Turkeys by the chair.

Turkeys by the table.

Turkeys everywhere!

Winter
Books

Bows on the bear.

Bows on the doll.

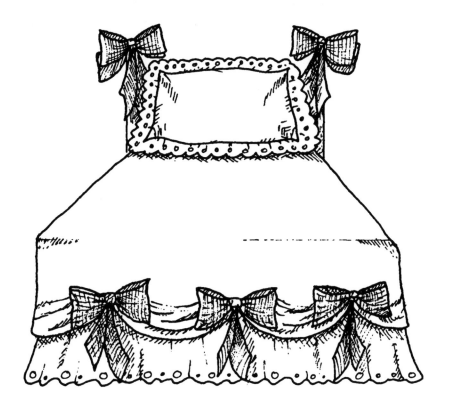

Bows on the bed.

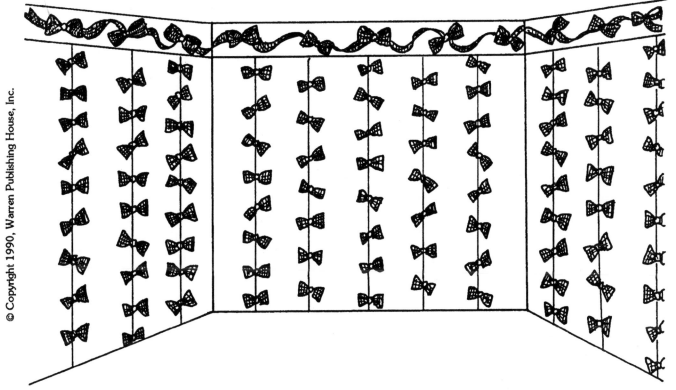

Bows on the wall.

Bows on the dress.

Bows on the socks.

Bows on the shoes.

Bows on the box.

Bows on the candles.

Bows on the stairs.

Bows on the door.

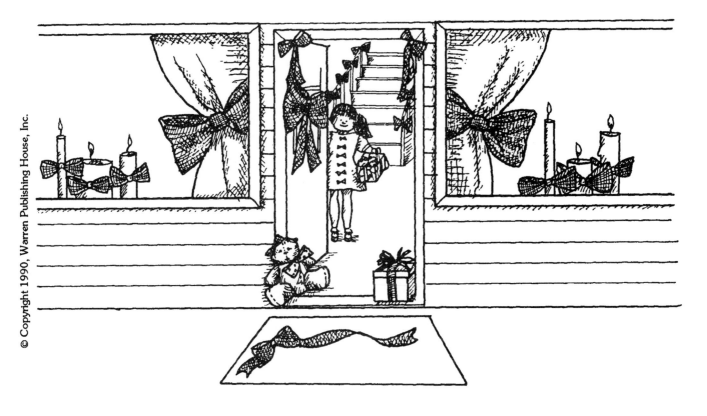

Bows everywhere!

Snow on the hill.

Snow on the tree.

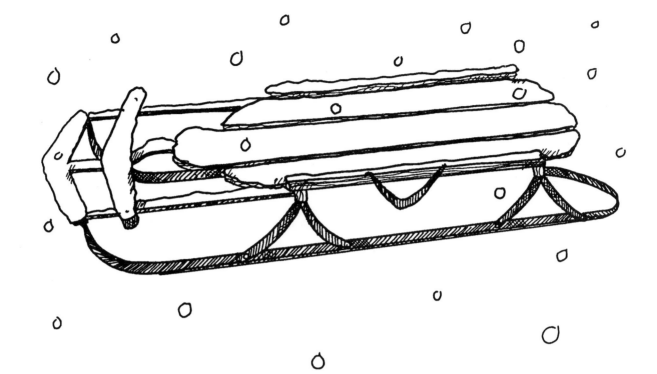

Snow on the sled.

Snow on me.

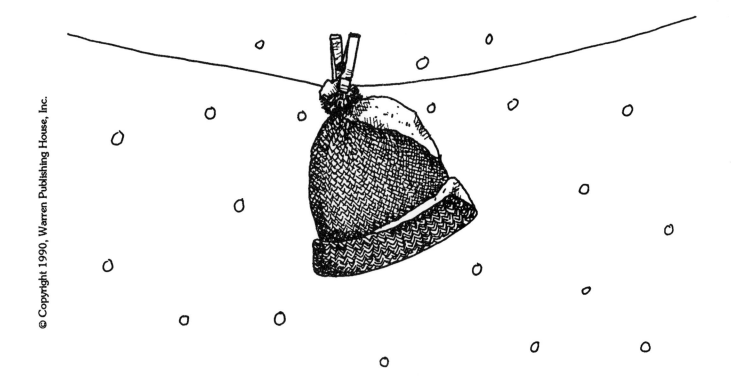

Snow on the hat.

Snow on the suit.

Snow on the mittens.

Snow on the boot.

Snow on the house.

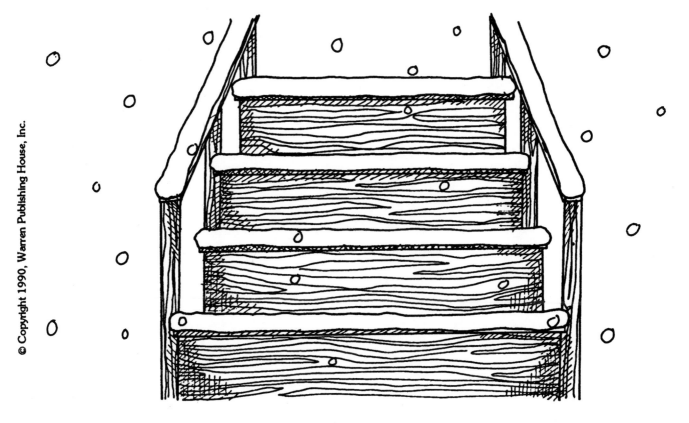

Snow on the stairs.

Snow on the window.

Snow everywhere!

Hearts on the mailbox.

Hearts on the door.

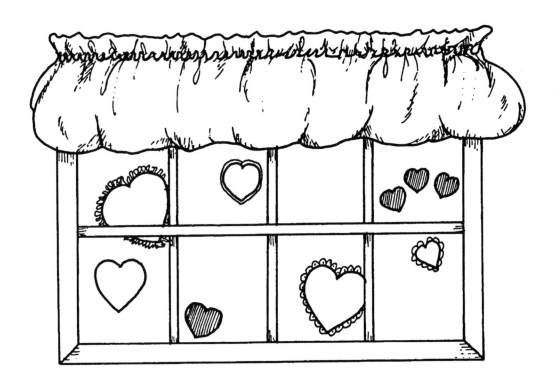

Hearts on the window.

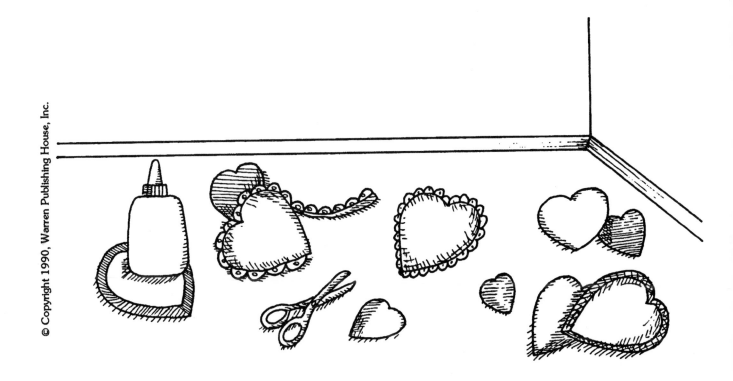

Hearts on the floor.

Hearts on the cake.

Hearts on the box.

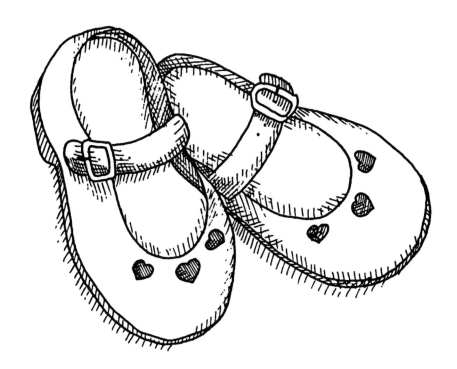

Hearts on the shoes.

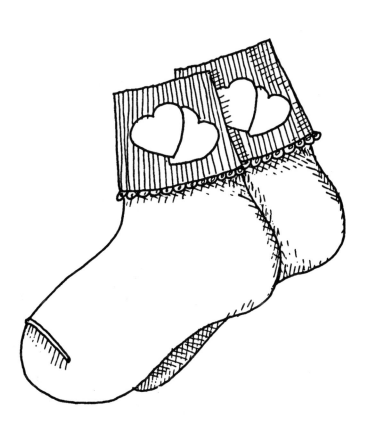

Hearts on the socks.

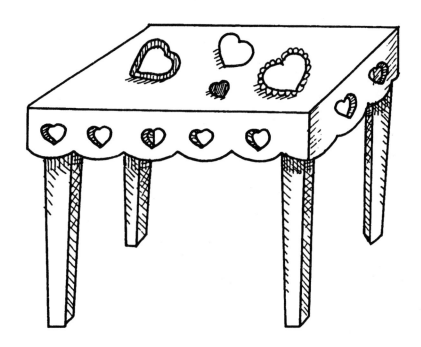

Hearts on the table.

Hearts on the chair.

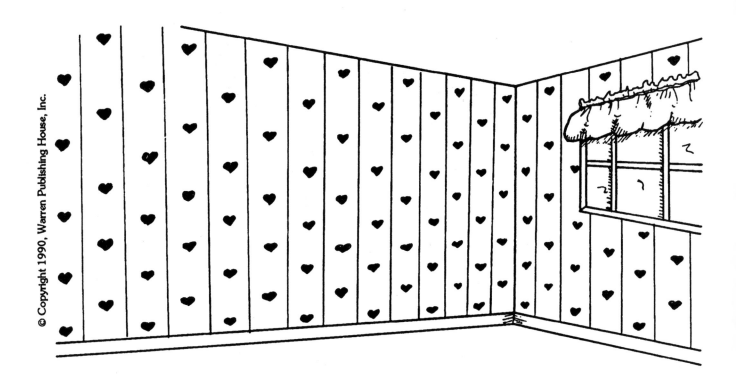

Hearts on the wall.

Hearts everywhere!

Spring
Books

Shamrocks on the coat.

Shamrocks on the hat.

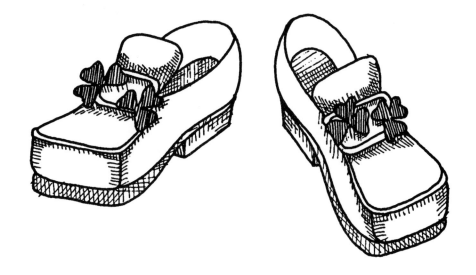

Shamrocks on the shoes.

Shamrocks on the cat.

Shamrocks on the window.

Shamrocks on the door.

Shamrocks on the walls.

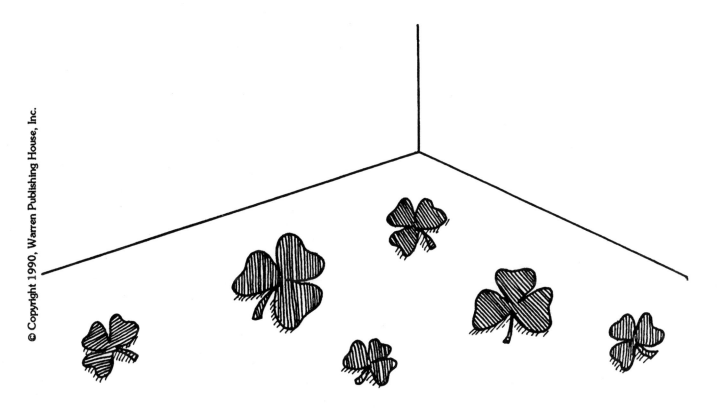

Shamrocks on the floor.

Shamrocks on the table.

Shamrocks on the chair.

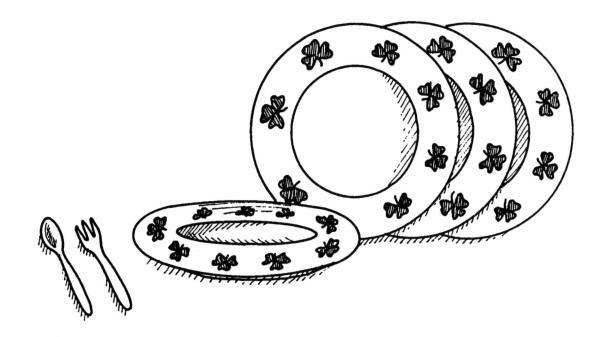

Shamrocks on the plates.

Shamrocks everywhere!

Rain on the cat.

Rain on the dog.

Rain on the pigs.

Rain on the frog.

Rain on the barn.

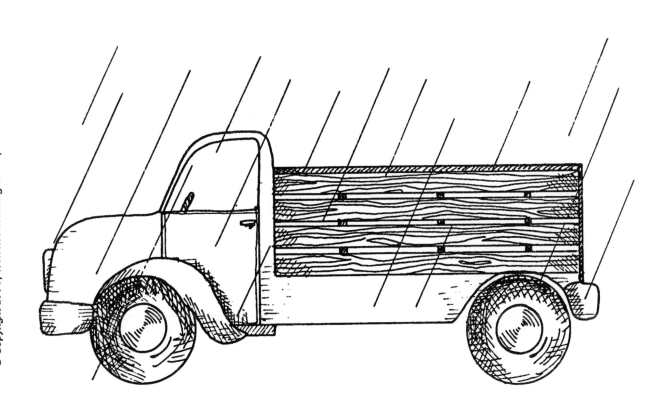

Rain on the truck.

Rain on the farmer.

Rain on the duck.

Rain on the colt.

Rain on the mare.

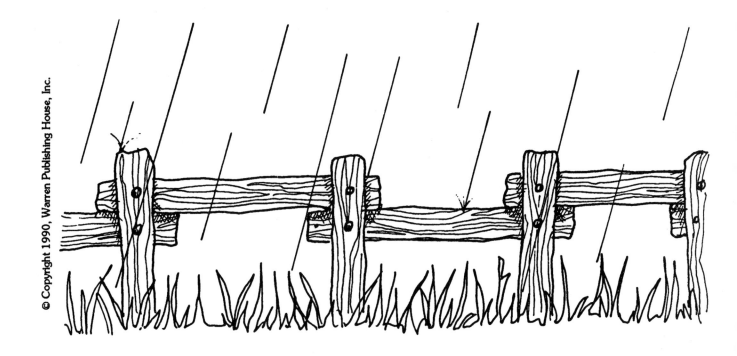

Rain on the fence.

Rain everywhere!

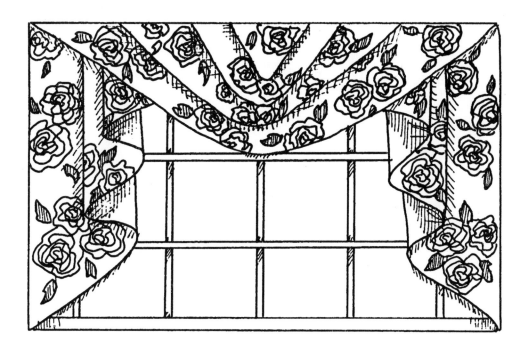

Flowers on the curtains.

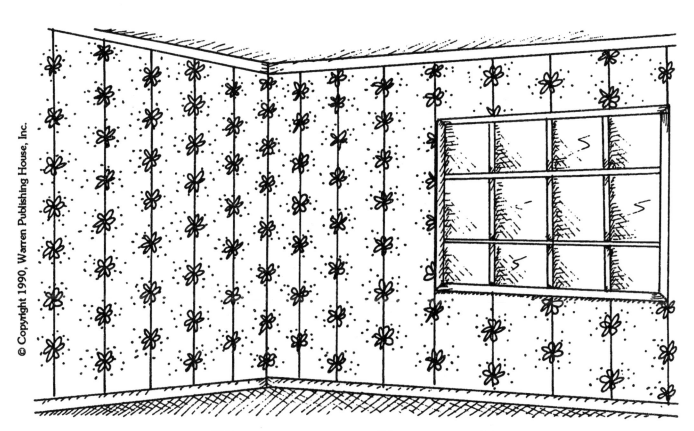

Flowers on the wall.

Flowers on the pillows.

Flowers on the doll.

Flowers on the towel.

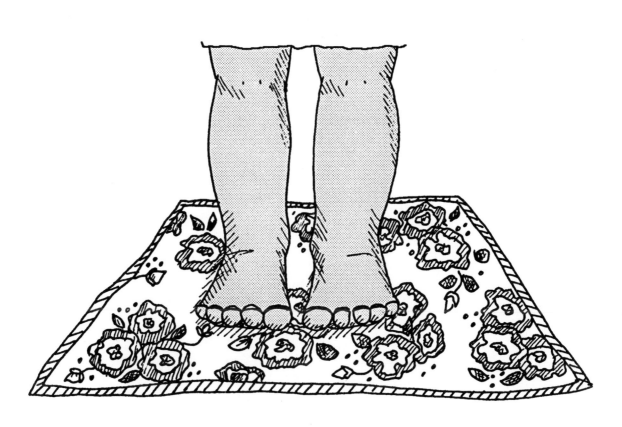

Flowers on the mat.

Flowers on the dress.

Flowers on the hat.

Flowers on the table.

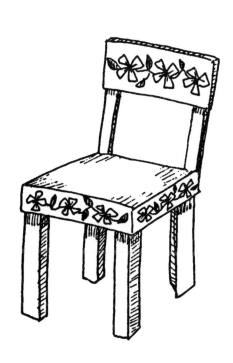

Flowers on the chair.

Flowers on the cup.

Flowers everywhere!

Summer
Books

Butterflies on the wagon.

Butterflies on the ball.

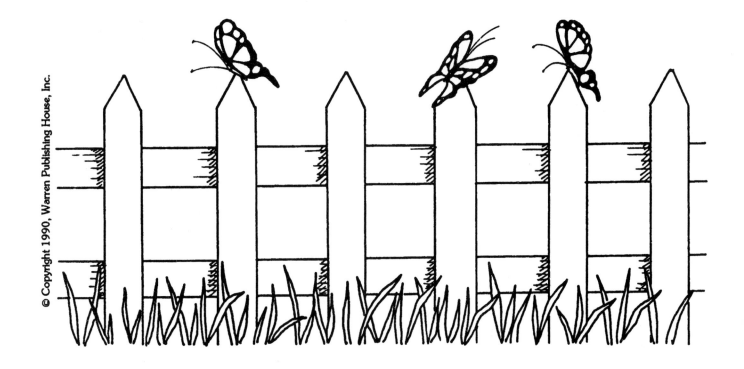

Butterflies on the fence.

Butterflies on the doll.

Butterflies on the flowers.

Butterflies on the grass.

Butterflies on the plate.

Butterflies on the glass.

Butterflies on the table.

Butterflies on the chair.

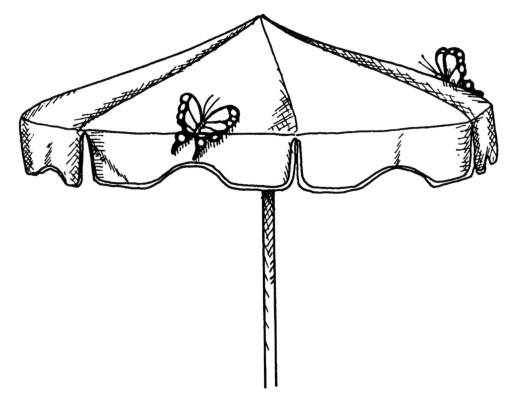

Butterflies on the umbrella.

Butterflies everywhere!

Flags on the cars.

Flags on the bikes.

Flags on the wagons.

Flags on the trikes.

Flags on the horses.

Flags on the floats.

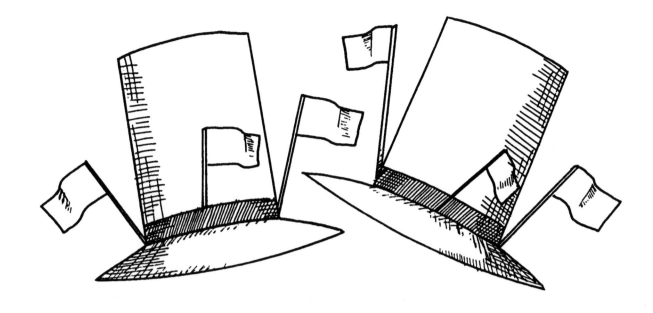

Flags on the hats.

Flags on the coats.

Flags on the drummers.

Flags on the bears.

Flags on the clowns.

Flags everywhere!

Sand on the beach.

Sand on the doll.

Sand on the book.

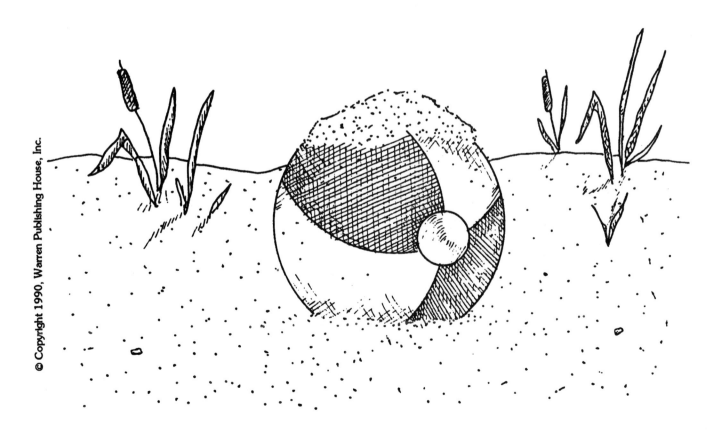

Sand on the ball.

Sand on the pail.

Sand on the box.

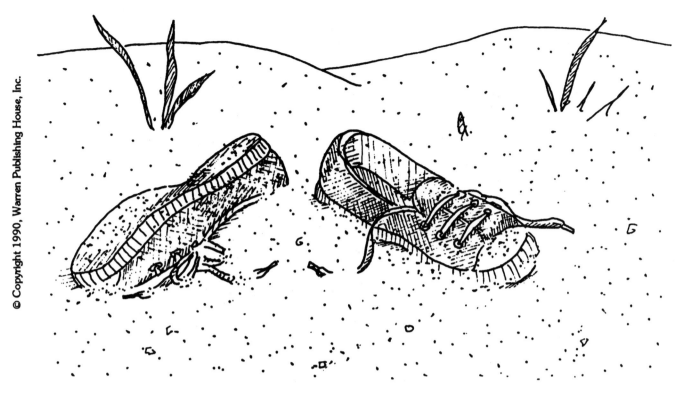

Sand on the shoes.

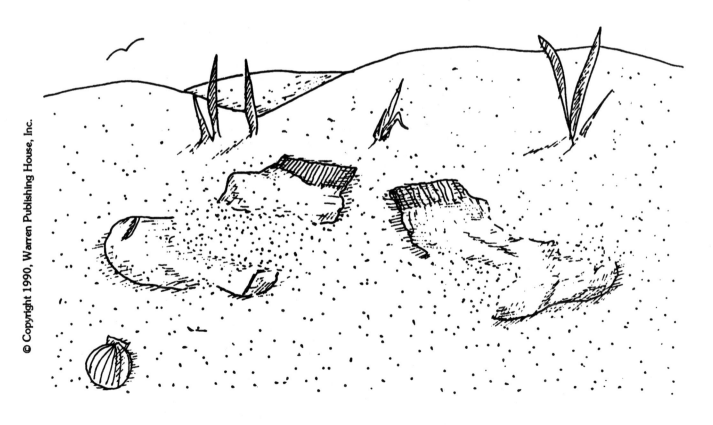

Sand on the socks.

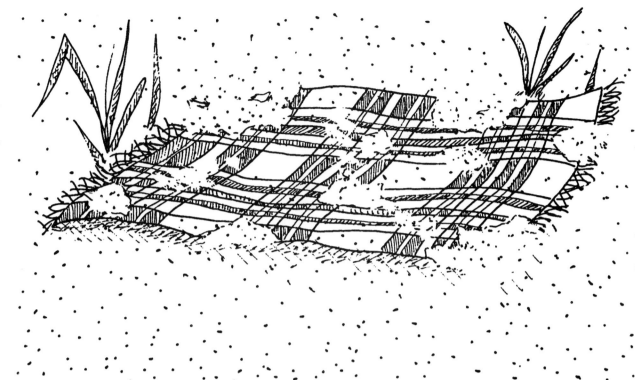

Sand on the blanket.

Sand on the bear.

Sand on the shovel.

Sand everywhere!

Totline® Newsletter

Activities, songs and new ideas to use right now are waiting for you in every issue!

Each issue puts the fun into teaching with 32 pages of challenging and creative activities for young children. Included are open-ended art activities, learning games, music, language and science activities plus 8 reproducible pattern pages.

Published bi-monthly.

Sample issue - $2.00

Super Snack News

Nutritious snack ideas, related songs, rhymes and activities

Sample issue - $2.00

- Teach young children health and nutrition through fun and creative activities.

- Use as a handout to involve parents in their children's education.

- Promote quality child care in the community with these handouts.

- Includes nutritious sugarless snacks, health tidbits, and developmentally appropriate activities.

- Includes CACFP information for most snacks.

With each subscription you are given the right to:

Make up to:
200 COPIES
per issue

Warren Publishing House, Inc. • P.O. Box 2250, Dept. Z • Everett, WA 98203

Totline® Books

PIGGYBACK® SONG SERIES

Piggyback® Songs

More Piggyback® Songs

Piggyback® Songs
for Infant s & Toddlers

Piggyback® Songs
in Praise of God

Piggyback® Songs
in Praise of Jesus

Holiday Piggyback® Songs

Animal Piggyback® Songs

Piggyback® Songs for School

Piggyback® Songs to Sign

1•2•3 SERIES

1•2•3 Art

1•2•3 Games

1•2•3 Colors

1•2•3 Puppets

1•2•3 Murals

1•2•3 Books

1•2•3 Reading & Writing

1•2•3 Rhymes, Stories & Songs

1•2•3 Math

1•2•3 Science

EXPLORING SERIES

Exploring Sand

Exploring Water

Exploring Wood

CELEBRATION SERIES

Small World Celebrations

Special Day Celebrations

Yankee Doodle
Birthday Celebrations

Great Big Holiday Celebrations

CUT & TELL SERIES

Scissor Stories for Fall

Scissor Stories for Winter

Scissor Stories for Spring

TEACHING TALE SERIES

Teeny-Tiny Folktales

Short-Short Stories

Mini-Mini Musicals

THEME-A-SAURUS® SERIES

Theme-A-Saurus®

Theme-A-Saurus® II

Toddler Theme-A-Saurus®

Alphabet Theme-A-Saurus®

Nursery Rhyme
Theme-A-Saurus®

Storytime Theme-A-Saurus®

TAKE-HOME SERIES

Alphabet & Number Rhymes

Color, Shape & Season Rhymes

Object Rhymes

Animal Rhymes

LEARNING & CARING ABOUT SERIES

Our World

Our Selves

Our Town

MIX & MATCH PATTERNS

Animal Patterns

Everyday Patterns

Holiday Patterns

Nature Patterns

ABC SERIES

ABC Space

ABC Farm

ABC Zoo

ABC Circus

1001 SERIES

1001 Teaching Props

OTHER

Super Snacks

Celebrating Childhood

Home Activity Booklet

23 Hands-On Workshops

**Totline books are available
at school supply stores
and parent/teacher stores,
or write for our free catalog.**

Warren Publishing House, Inc. • P.O. Box 2250, Dept. B • Everett, WA 98203